Beneath the Horse's Eye

Poems by

Dale Jacobs

Published by Spotted Cow Press
4216 - 121 Street, Edmonton, Alberta T6J 1Y8
www.spottedcowpress.ab.ca

ISBN 0-9694665-3-6

Cover photograph by Jerome Martin.

For my parents

ACKNOWLEDGMENTS

Some of the poems in this collection first appeared in the following magazines: *Fan Magazine, The Flint Hills Review, The MacGuffin, Main Street Rag Poetry Journal, Pink Cadillac Review, Plainsongs, Poet Lore, Poetry Motel Wallpaper Broadside Series, South Dakota Review,* and *Thorny Locust.*

Some of these poems were published in *Signs Flashing,* a limited-edition chapbook published by *Ultima Obscura Press.*

I would like to thank Heidi Jacobs for her love and support, Jerome, Merle, Melanie, and Lu at *Spotted Cow Press,* and the members of the Thursday Night Writers' Group.

CONTENTS

ONE

TWO

THREE

FOUR

ONE

THE SQUARE ROOT OF LIVING

Miles to the gallon, blocks to and from work, shopping days
left until Christmas, 123 days without an accident posted

proudly in my mechanic's shop, the typology of statistics
concrete in the everyday, how many, how far, how long,

elementary equations, the clock ticks, sixty and twenty-four
equal one. Waiting in the lobby these digits click in my mind

and I wonder whether more imports or domestics, more cash
or credit, and if there are more people who also wonder,

this numbers game that I play with myself, one, two, three,
no wonder I loved to watch the Count on Sesame Street

sitting there in front of my parents' old black and white tv
counting stuffed animals, cows, books. I heard on NPR

today order comes from chaos, a complex numerology,
the patterns of statistics somehow separating experience

into sense. I marvel at the implied lack of randomness,
counting the number of times the announcer says chaos.

WHAT WE DID

We were all the same, small town kids with too much
time on our hands. Summer days we would roam
dirt streets, look for trouble, but not too much,
just enough to ease the boredom a little, make us
forget for a while there was nothing to do.
We would play knock-a-door-ginger, bang on
the doors of old people, leave vague notes,
nasty somehow, or so we thought. Hide behind
hedges to see their faces, annoyed or angry sometimes,
mostly understanding why we did it, young and bored
once too. Sometimes, though, we would take it further
just to get back the rush. Synchronize
imaginations. Out through basement windows.
Rendevous at one. Firecrackers, stink bombs, sneakers
laced, matches ready, we would head for the bar. Open
the door, toss, run. Not too fast — let them see
your back. Through streets, alleys, backyards
burned in our minds, just danger enough, a shot
of adrenaline straight to the heart. Like the times
we heard the train whistle four or five blocks
from the tracks, dropped what we were doing and ran,
needing to make it to the other side before it passed.
Across the highway, through the ditch. Just a little faster.
Still got time. Look back. Train passes.
Heart pounds.

FEVER DREAMS

fever dreams of snow
crunching underfoot
soles of my boots carving
a path home lines
on a map obscured by
drifts of white like
the chocolate we used
to break with our coffee
as we endlessly argued
the relative merits of
snow and rain
us warm and dry
Columbian coffee and
Belgian chocolate
easing the Canadian
sense of hardship that
pushed us together
you with that unkempt
smile under your beard
across from me as I turned
the white of my cup
in on itself
the crush of students on
either side swarming
to English or Biology

relations between humans
and the world examined
through lenses partial and
unfamiliar like trying to solve
a jigsaw puzzle with no box
to tell you that there is a fit
between the background
pieces of rain and snow

STATIC

Switchin' over to AM,
Searchin' for a truer sound.
— Son Volt, "Windfall"

It's enough to drive, Nebraska highways
stretched to a distant horizon we may
never reach. Across another county line,
Patsy Cline sings "Walking After Midnight,"

my parents' kitchen and Bev Munroe's talk on
CFCW. *Pass the milk, can I have some more*
juice, out in the moonlight just like we used
to do. My parents eat toast, the jam on

the edge of their plates, no crumbs seep into
sealed jars of raspberry jam, last year's preserves
lined on a shelf in the cold room. *That's just*
my way of saying I love you. A few minutes

until the schoolbus comes, across the street,
then down another highway, home already
in the rearview mirror. *I stopped to see*
a weeping willow cryin' on his pillow,

maybe he's cryin' for me. The station
fades in and out, an increase in the static.
The hands of their old clock move
over dark wood while they face each

other across the table. Alberta morning.
My father's fingers search for the last
crumbs on his plate. I raise the styrofoam
to my lips, search Nebraska fields for signs

of life, hum an old song to myself. *I'm so
lonesome I could cry.* It's hard to drive
without music, without rhythm and melody
and their voices across the table.

PRELUDE

Third to second to first,
around the horn,
eyes touching
the curve of the ball,
catch, set, fire,
as weathered green slats
on the third base side
caress my back.
Beside me an old woman
readies a scorecard,
to encode the game
in a script of statistics,
gnarled hands eager
to author a double play
6-4-3,
short to second to first.
To my left the chair
awaits my companion,
popcorn and lemonade
(her ballpark provisions)
tucked in arms that encircle
knees when it gets too cold
in the late innings.
Coors Beer Coors Beer here.

A vendor's baritone,
familiar face creased
with sweat and age,
sun setting on the Marlboro Man,
lights burning
red to yellow to white,
grounds' crew massaging
hard-worked soil,
relieving the knots
that make grounders hitch,
error charged to the infielder
dutifully recorded
on an old woman's card.
And then all rise
for the singing of the Anthem,
the rest of the crowd
filling in.

AUBADE

You ask what makes the sumac shine
while the red of the stars echoes clear across

our laughter, the coming Nebraska morning
dark with dew, light with the crickets' song.

Across to the east, the first light dawns in
our neighbors' window, day's early greeting

or night's difficult farewell. It's all a matter of
desperate whispers, the beginning or the end

of love's daily revolution, lovers under cover of
conversation, private lives that run deeper than

who we are with other people. I imagine them
rising together, their first words echoing our last,

the coming of the morning their blessing and our
curse. Then the red begins to streak across your

face, the glow heavy on your cheek, and I know
the sumac's shine is gone for us but not for them.

SADDLE

Her saddle sits in the middle of the study's floor,
upended, Murphy's oil soap worked into the black
leather pores, a caress of moisture worked hard
into months of neglect. Her horse is retired,
too old at twenty-one for dressage or the trails,
Nebraska heat and flies as much as he can handle
most days, as much as she expects him to handle.

His name is Country Gentleman — a dozen years and still
her friend, confidante, he is the oldest horse in the pasture,
finished with shows, but carefully brushed and tended,
retired but still part of her life. He knows more than
he can ever communicate, more than most of her
friends, about this woman, grown from the girl who
needed help to mount his back, her English saddle.

They have cantered together on Edmonton river
trails, danced dressage, galloped through fields,
the saddle their connection to each other, flesh
fused in the grain of the leather. Their lives intersect,
this horse and this woman, each dependent on the
other, each wishing for the day they will meet once
more in the saddle, flesh to flesh, merged in the ride.

BONE

At twenty-five I chose the perfect bone,
hard china cream edged with exact

geometry. There could be no doubt in
the absolute strength of those lines

captured within the delicate ring of gold,
intricate movements of blue on beige,

the connection of points in their proper
lineage. Your fingers touched my arm,

confirmed that the shortest path between
two people is a straight line; each counts

on the other and in the equation a pattern
emerges. We turned cups in our hands,

your light caress a calm assurance we
made the right choice, bred in the bone.

ALL HE EVER SAW

Ordinary eternal machinery is like the grinding of the stars.
—Leonard Cohen, Beautiful Losers

Numbers on the clock blaze red, the colon
blinks between the 2 and the 18, off and on,
the knowing wink of the metronome gathers
him inside, ordinary in his bed, covers splayed,
the happenstance of wakefulness.

As July warmth floods over him, over every
inch of his efficiency, his thoughts mingle
with the eternal rustle of the wind and paper
falling softly on his desk, tomorrow, forever,
again, blink, blink.

The 2 becomes 3 and he makes lists, a habit
he once thought would help him sleep,
all the girls he ever dated, all the Brando movies
he ever saw, all the parts of life that don't add up
to anything but pieces of machinery.

Somewhere between *Superman* and *Don Juan
Demarco,* he slips into dream, time, night,
and the everyday grind to a halt and he floats
breathless, waves of stars washing over him,
ordinary, eternal, machinery.

CALL

Always I give myself
over to assurance,
air cushion finish,
round corners tracing
my hand, resilient touch
a siren's call, the chaos
and order inherent in a deck,
space for the game
overlaid with the rush,
the possibility, the renewal
of each hand, obscure
destinies made actual
with the turn of a card, never
quite drawing to an inside
straight, house games,
hours spent searching
faces, endless clatter of smoke
odors of speech lingering
before the odds of a flush
across the table, too much
for the three ladies I have
in my hand, the spirit of the game
lifting me in a rush of symbols,
coins dancing across our table,
hands shuffling back and forth.

CONNECT

I never knew what love was until I watched him
play connect the dots on the huge map that hung
above his bed, pins in red, green, blue, orange
tracing her path through Dublin, Nice, Florence,
Trieste. I would follow the trail of sound, Elvis
Costello or the Violent Femmes, and see him
traveling, pins pressed hard into cork, imprint of her
lips on his own and I would have to knock hard
to be heard above his thoughts. Before he turned
he would feign concentration on an imaginary
guitar, tuning and strumming for my benefit,
the motion of the music replacing the stillness
of his figure imposed on the map.

He would offer me a drink from the old yellow newspaper
box liquor cabinet, always gin, Tanqueray in its green
bottle taken from its place next to the Glen Fiddich. And then
he would begin to talk about her, never admitting that he
missed her, but telling me instead how she had danced at
the Höfbrauhaus, floated through Venice, sent him a postcard
of Renoir's *Le Moulin de la Gâlette.* Sometimes we would discuss
what we wanted to see in Europe, but most of the time I just
listened to him not missing her.

Across the calender that hung next to the map he marked off the days until the next phone call, always Thursday, always eight o'clock, Mountain Standard Time, though he always knew her time too. After he would retreat to his weekly glass of Glen Fiddich, reading over her letters again, never missing her, of course, just connecting a couple of more dots with a press of his finger.

GREASEWOOD

I.

Highway 25 whizzing beneath the wheels
of the rented Buick, the passenger seat
perspective is unfamiliar to me.
The desert flashes at the sides of my
vision, cactus, yucca, greasewood, a high
speed blur of vegetation, individual plants
recede into an Interstate landscape
marking the miles to Las Cruces.
No one remembers how we decided
on New Mexico. One day it just happened
and here we are, Heidi and her mother in
the back seat as her father taps the wheel,
asks me how things are in Lincoln.

II.

Sometimes at stop lights on O Street I will
suddenly realize I'm in Nebraska and I can't
remember any moment of decision, but then
the light is green and I'm driving again, focused
on the road ahead, objects in the mirror fading,
blending into the haze of a Nebraska night.

III.

I stare at the desert, straining to capture
a single cactus, to gauge my movement
against that fixed point of reference,
dizzying, impossible, I'm forced to focus
inside the glass. I'm staring back, reflected,
refracted, partial, a silhouette etched
momentarily before receding into its own
private landscape.

IV.

At night, eyes closed, I think of prior movements,
attempt to reconstruct the route that led me from
Alberta to Nebraska, from Amisk to graduate school,
but it's a blur, a cascade of choices
I can no longer trace back to the source.
Only the larger picture emerges, details merge
together, a thousand decisions propel me to
this street, this life. But even the pauses run
faster than the speed of contemplation and leave
me unable to separate the ends from the means.

V.

In the desert there are no stop lights, only miles
of open thought, the passenger seat of a rented Buick,
all the decisions that led us to Las Cruces, and time
to teach myself to focus on a single
greasewood. Dizzying, but not impossible.

CONFESSION

Saturday and Sunday football never made me want to strap
on shoulder pads, hurl my body at oncoming players,
invent myself running along the curve of the grass,
a down field block from the split end and one man to
beat for a touchdown. Instead I was anointed by
a senior tailback under a Friday night sky.

I only saw him play once, on a cool September night,
afternoon shading into evening. Cheerleaders huddled
under varsity jackets, kids from the elementary school
wrestled behind the bleachers, their parents watched
older sons, yelled encouragement, caught up with
other parents, sometimes friends and sometimes not,
connected then by school, children, and 'Bolts' football.

For weeks after, I arose every Saturday, carried the sports
section to the window seat of my living room, replayed
every run he made — off tackles, sweeps, options, draws.
The fans came to see him every Friday night, but I could
only imagine another yard, another touchdown through
the distance of words. The beauty was too personal,
too fleeting, the terrible energy of a moment
I could never recapture.

I stood at the back of the home bleachers, a peripheral
fan cradling hot chocolate against the Nebraska chill,
and could see him cut back against his blocking, move
to the hole in the line, break the linebacker's grip on
his legs, stutter step past a closing safety, sprint for
another touchdown. Every touch of the ball seemed
eight yards, legs churning, cleats turning clumps
of sod, brown pulp replacing the field's brilliant green.
Whenever the guard pulled to the left, he would follow,
defensive line clearing like mist on a crisp autumn morning,
linebacker's breath rising from his face mask, a single
penitent awaiting the benediction of the running back,
the perfect absolution of contact.

TWO

HOLDING THE CORNER

the horn of the rhino dragged across
my palm exposing the patterns of its
smooth underbelly wooden figurines
and my Aunt smooth in her stately blue
dress and perfect white hair as her soft
voice told me the story I held in my hands

and the rhinoceros screamed in sorrow
as she saw her mate fall under the enormous
weight of the world's corner and the rhinoceros
knew that she had to decide between her
beloved and the animals who ran in panic
about her and she said goodbye to her mate
and pulled up the corner of the world as
tears streaked her horn

in my Aunt's eye was also a tear and I
knew the story was over my Aunt then
turning to her sister leaving me with the
mahogany rhino cradled in my arms fingers
gently touching the story she had left for me

later I would remember the feel of the rhino's
skin against my own skin and the radiant
sadness of my Aunt's face as she remembered
what she had lost and the corner of the world
she had supported

years later when I saw Dühren's woodcut
I thought of my Aunt and the story of
the rhinoceros I closed the book and
replaced its hard scales with the visage of my
Aunt and the sound of her words and the wet
horn of the rhino dragging across my palm

P(R)OEM

A conversation overheard,
my prying ears straining
against all sense of propriety,
moving closer, pulling away,
coffee house voyeur,
words channelled from ear to pen,

their reality becoming my fiction.
And I wonder whose fiction I am
becoming as I sit here scribbling,
that strange writer on page 57
sitting alone drinking espresso,
rolling cigarettes, talking to himself,
distraction or minor character

in a novel by somebody else.
Over by the window, light playing
in the folds of his coat, heavy white mug
untouched word scraps settling
over him, ash grey, black book marks,
a poem writing itself.

READING THE SIGNS

It was raining the day I asked my father
about that old catcher's mitt we had never
spoken about before — never in all those years
of Dave Van Horne and Duke Snider
and the Expos on CBC from the old Jarry Park,
never in the few times we played catch when
I was a kid, never in all those conversations
about the Blue Jays when there was nothing
else to say. We never talked about it, but I had
seen him handle that glove, his fingers caressing
the dark leather, his right hand beating a pocket
too small to cover the ball's bright red stitches.
Let's go to the basement and find it, he said.
I followed in silence, down the stairs, through
our past, my father's step sure and deliberate.
As he switched on the light, I could see the sheen
of the leather on the shelf where I knew it would be.
My Dad gave me this glove in 1923 — I was eight
years old — I want you to have it. He handed me
the glove and smiled as I put it on and slammed
my fist into its pocket.

CALLING FROM BROKEN BOW

Suitcase spilled on the bed, I slump
down in the motel chair, exhausted by
the Nissan's hurried miles, our progress
registered in backseat artifacts —
Coke cans, sunflower seeds, Twix wrappers.
Knowing he is anxious for my call,
I raise the receiver to my ear, awaiting his
voice on the other end of the line.

Dad? Is that you?

He answers and I wait
for the question
I know is sure to follow.

The drive? It went pretty well.

He wants to know which way we came,
which roads we travelled, what country we saw.
So I tell our day's journey —
roads, sights, weather —
just as I had for countless
other trips, comforted by the familiar
rhythm of query and answer,
by his voice
at the other end of the line.

Yeah, you're right, it's a long way
from Amisk to Broken Bow

I picture him there in his black
work shirt, in his old black chair,
gently pressing the receiver to his ear,
straining to hear my answers over
the roar of miles.

State 83 from Bismark to Thedford, all the way
through North Dakota, South Dakota, and
Nebraska. Then we got on 2 and took it to
Broken Bow.

After our conversation is over, he will
retrace my steps, filling the spaces,
transforming the red and blue lines
into real stretches of road
with real scenery and real weather,
following me in the two-dimensions
of map space, an unseen presence that watches,
but never intrudes, because he understands
the journey.

We should be in Lincoln by early afternoon and
then I guess we'll start looking for an apartment.

As I replace the receiver in its cradle,
I wonder what Dad thinks
of my going, of my reasons.
Lincoln, too, is a long way from Amisk.

THE SPACE TO TRY

I have been here before, but not with you.
Chicago, under the El, pawnshops and bars
tempt me — *Quick Cash Happy Hour*
Stereos Budweiser — the neon flash lights
the way of past trips, Dave or Pete and I
loose in the big city, imagining that we
had found its underbelly in the shadow
of the El. One dark room to another, drunk
on what we had made of Chicago, not
the city you see today, your vision clouded
differently than mine, intoxicated by your
own expectations of place.

You couldn't hide your surprise, March grey
slanting through the skylight, one of our first
talks, the awkward give and take of getting to
know each other not yet dissipated — twice
I had been to Chicago and never visited
the Art Institute, world renowned, you said,
images you knew only in facsimile, slides
never replacing the paintings themselves.
As I looked at you, listened to your voice, I was
scared of what you made of me, ball games
and bars outweighing art — our worlds seemed
so distant, I didn't know if we could make the
space to even try on what mattered to the other.

You tease me now about missing the Art Institute
those times before, our days together now tripping
into a life, the guts of our worlds mixed and overlapping.
Today we walk to see Seurat and Rosetti, on another
it will be Alomar and Carter. You squeeze my hand,
point to lions that I had passed without any thought.
Yes, I have been here before, but not with you.

FLORAL ARRANGEMENT

In *Margo's* I surveyed the color of roses —
red, white, cream — until I settled on black
for our first date. I liked the dark sheen,
petals the color of warm blood, circling
a core too deep for anyone to reach.

Labels insisted the names of the other
flowers in the case, camellias, orchids,
gladiolas, gardenias, but I chose the black
rose to drape across stark white Italian linen.

The perfect black of the rose's lines glossed
the symbology of that species and genus,
the language of flowers which I cannot speak,
the grammar hidden from me then under
layers of practicality or aesthetics.

Five years and a thousand miles from
Margo's I search for another black rose,
but only the red remains, rows of flowers
that speak to others but not to me.

Over coffee I lay the red across Heidi's
hand, tell her I wish it could be a deeper
shade, another color, but she holds her
finger to my lips, tells me she's always
known the rarity of a black rose.

GARDEN

Tawny hair and skin worn
like clothes that
don't quite fit,
thrift store castoffs
of another world.

Tending her roses,
peonies, asters, all
encircling our building,
marking the compass
of her world, I see
her standing,
home and not home
in a foreign land
with a foreign tongue.

Around her my words fail
and I manage only to blurt
that the flowers are lovely.
From my country,
she beams,
eyes sparkling, dancing
as she points to the plot
of unknown flowers.

As I slide behind
the wheel of my car,
she moves away,
an old woman again,
tawny hair and skin worn
like memories
of home.

TRIPTYCH

preacher framed between
crucifix and attendance board
at the front of
our old church
gravel voice trailing
repentance from his
worn blue vest
straddling salvation for
all and the numbering
of the saved the sinners
of course were too
numerous to mention
against black cardboard
white numbers starkly
aligned in four slots
covered by gently
slanting eaves that
sheltered it like a crèche
barometer of our
church's holiness

in worn pews i prayed
that extra zeroes
would appear like
loaves multiplying

and i dreamed a floor
littered with black
squares inlaid with
white numbers

and i watched
for any change in
the shrine or the man but
saw only Christ's head
crumpled to his breast

LOST SHAKER OF SALT

I was the one who spotted it, tucked close
into the dirty white front of the building,
just off Massachussets, not quite to New
Hampshire, hidden but for the red neon
burning *Bud* into the night. Six of us
piled in from the November cold, both
blocks since the last bar chilling us through
fall jackets, through the push of Kansas wind.

It was Key Largo in the flat of Kansas, a mirage,
painted palm trees and fishing nets strung
low, juke box CDs encased in glass like water
over silver baubles, pirate's booty to relieve us
of our money — *five plays for a dollar, thirty*
plays for five. Music flowed from the discs,
the breeze of dancers grew, washing over
us, first *Jungle Boogie,* then *Kung Fu Fightin',*
the Sandbar that night an oasis of another decade.

Later we danced on the bar, two at a time —
no one cared, the bartenders even helped
us up — too many Marguerítas and Bahama
Mamas swirling in clear plastic tanks
along the wall, a department store snack
bar gone bad, too much Jimmy Buffet,
sixteen CDs and every time we played
a song someone bumped the machine
until it played *Cheeseburger in Paradise.*

Back in Nebraska we started to ask other
people who knew that Kansas town if
they had ever heard of the place, just off
Manhattan or was it Massachussets, you know,
the keys of the Midwest. No one knew it
but us, as if a little rift in time had opened
and the bar just appeared, the Sandbar
our *Brigadoon,* Jimmy Buffet our Gene Kelly
just lookin' for his lost shaker of salt.

THE HITTER'S GEOMETRY

Until 1930, a fair ball that bounced into the bleachers was scored as a ground-rule homerun. At the end of the 1930 season, the National League ruled that any such hit would be scored as a ground-rule double.

Imagine how it feels as it leaves the bat.
Not the solid contact between ball and
muscle or the slow trot to first and around

the scorecard, eyes extended to the park's
horizon. More like skipping a stone across the
water, your arm too tired or weak to reach

the other side all at once, the force of the arc
turned in on itself, straightened to a four-base
line drive. The ball just beyond the out

stretched glove of the fielder hits the hard
grass of late summer, patches of brown
hiding the possibility of green, spins forward

towards the wall, ricochets on sun-dried wood.
Al Lopez was one of the last to feel that
hope of a top-spin carom, off the grass in

left and into the bleacher corner. The Dodgers'
catcher lined the shot, whirling, spinning over the
head of Bob Meusel, Ebbets Field sun high

over a Brooklyn sky. Maybe he practiced putting
spin on the ball, aiming at the patch of grass in
left that took all the sun. Maybe he was lucky.

That day the hope of a home run was still
alive for everyone who hit without power,
the chance for a spot of hard grass, an extra

bounce slowing the hitter's gait to familiar
circling, the final time around the bases.

DESIGNATED HITTER

All the great names are gone —
the Great Bambino, the Sultan
of Swat, the Bronx Bomber —
though Berman tries every night
on ESPN, sportscaster's banter,
puns flying like balls out of batting
practice, a few landing on the warning
track, most hooking foul into the seats.
In the 90's nicknames don't stick,
no legends in name, no appellations,
glory dripping from the tongues of fans.
But George Herman Ruth was bigger
than his name, a man who couldn't
be contained in first, middle, and last,
the myth growing up around him —
the home runs, the called shot,
his swing changing the game forever —
enveloping, blurring the sacred
and the profane, he remained
separate from us in name and stature.
Maybe now we know too much to name
our heroes, their every mis-step splashed
across the sports section, late night gossip
mixed with sportscast scores, tabloid names
replacing field designations. Maybe Ruth
was named and renamed because we never
really knew him and maybe it was better that way.

RONDEL

The craft of loving is opaque at best.
Nobody knew what the two of them meant —
if it was really profound or words bent
around saucers of tea, flaunted to guests.

The pure function of each cup was their test
metaphor of love — hidden warmth, potent —
the craft of loving is opaque. At best
nobody knew what the two of them meant

to each other — their couple's smile, some jest
known only to them. The heart's dominant
need: another heart, somewhere else to vent
the laughter, the coiled steam within the breast.

The craft of loving is opaque at best.

ON CHILDREN

Babies have a way of sneaking up
on you when you least expect it —
first one friend, then another, one,
two, even three babies each. Baby
showers, christenings, one more Winnie
the Pooh toy to buy and then the inevitable
question: *So, when are the two of you having*

a small one of your own? And I don't know what
to say to this endless query. *Never* ? That seems
so harsh and final. *Someday* ? That seems so false.
I don't know ? Maybe true, but it won't be enough
for them. Sometimes I try to catch Heidi's eye, to see
if she's heard, sometimes I take a drink of the coffee
or wine I've been handed. Usually I make a joke,
deflecting the conversation back to them and
their children, crawling along the carpet, crying,
laughing, eating, waiting to be born.

THREE

REPLAY

At fifteen Monday broke my heart.
All I could do was sit and watch
as the ball streaked toward the fence,
rising, Rogers' fastball too high in the zone
and it was gone. None of us wanted
to believe it as we watched that small tv
in the middle of Alberta, thousands of miles
from Montreal, from a home run that
I can't forget.

The Expos came to bat, but I knew
it was over, Fernando on the hill
and the image of white still drifting over
the heads of Dawson and Raines.
As I watched the Dodgers celebrate,
Mr. Moen switched off the tv and walked
out the door, leaving the silence
of that classroom and his students.
Time had stopped that day for all of us,
the Expos in the NLCS more important
than math or biology or english,
the whole country hanging on every pitch.
Now in that silent room I could hear the click
of tvs being switched off all over Canada,
the CBC switching to a program already in progress.

The Dodgers went on to win the Series —
I know because I saw it in the box scores
when I returned from playing ball with friends,
arguing over who got to be Gary Carter,
stepping to the plate in the bottom of the ninth,
Dawson on second and a belt-high fastball
that keeps rising off the bat, higher and higher,
over the fence in left.

SKIN

for Donna

Her husband can no longer touch
the skin that haunts her body, now
drawn taut across her frame. Glassy
tension. A too tight drum ready to
snap and release. Under the skin
she floats, suppresses the pain
of touch, releases herself from
herself, spirals down, away from
the hurt, into the core of her body,
beneath the increasing surface
tension.

I picture this withdrawal, this woman
whose skin has betrayed her, too
contracted to contain the person she was,
shrunk, as if at 36 her life had closed in on
her and she must have thought,
Why?

She and I were never close but her
death haunts me, rattles against
my memories of her: her smile, that
summer day I sat with them in the *Grinder*
eating potato skins and drinking draft beer,
his proposal to her in the *Sun,* her answer,
pictures of her on his office desk, both of
them there at my own wedding. They
loved and at the end couldn't even hold
hands, could speak only with their eyes
or with words that can never say enough.

WHITE ON WHITE

The figures glide silently.
Spin. Swirl.
Ghost figures dance with stretchers.
Bags of clear fluid, tubes extended,
waiting arms of inmates,
wheeled beside, tethered.
Wheelchairs, alien machines,
meld into one,
float through a dance
without meaning.

The dance dissolves.

I stare at the piece of paper in my hand,
at the ink smudged with my sweat,
her room number barely legible,
hurriedly copied when the call came.
She is here.
I force myself to walk on,
the sickening smells of sterility combine,
bring me to the edge of nausea.

Cancer ward.
I pull up abruptly.
Cancer.
She can't have cancer.
I know, though, that she does,
that she is lying in a bed in that ward.
Cancer ward.

I knock, wondering if she's conscious,
knowing, yet not knowing what to expect.
There is someone in the bed, but it's not her.
It's a trick, this isn't her,
this isn't my mother, this woman with tubes that
jut from her at strange angles.
It's a ghost-image of my mother,
with all the colour, all the life removed,
white like the walls,
sterile like the place itself.

Sliding into the chair, next to her bed,
I pray for colour.

WHAT WE SAW

Chalk stains on the back of Mr.Currie's
brown corduroy jacket His looping hand

across the board Desks that read
FH LOVES JD and CURRIE SUCKS

Books pencilled with answers and dirty
words Broken pieces of last year's wire

art projects Bathroom fights Red stains
where lip met porcelain The leather

strap pulled from a teacher's desk
The pain it caused Yellow buses

Green naugahyde seats Dust Snow
angels Rusted pickups and cars pitted

by gravel Turret and Sportsman
cigarettes pulled from heavy fall coats

Tackle football Playground fights
Baseball without enough players

Circumstantial friends Waves
of grass in an Alberta wind

LIVING ROOM

Slouched in his familiar chair,
rough skin sun-darkened,
loose on a frame unaccustomed
to not working, to being inside,
alone, he is there, t.v. blaring
in the small room of the living.

Drinking coffee in Lincoln, Nebraska
I picture my father in that chair,
the one that's held him since he retired,
cataract operations driving him inside
from the farm to days
living in that small room.

Twenty years he has sat in that chair
in a town too small for me,
too big for him, a never land
for us both, he told me
to get away before I was trapped, only
room there for small living.

What is he thinking as he sits
watching the farms die as he recedes,
grows quieter, he and mom
in a house built for three,
but too large for two, too much
room for living in that small space.

All those years growing up
he sat there, silent, unspeaking,
I love him and don't even know him,
neither`of us able to tell the other
what those years meant
in the small room of the living.

a day in the life

the trim of your beard washing the white
porcelain swirling remnants of you
your image in the glass reflecting
a face you don't know like the cat
watching the animal in the stove glass
no scent of familiarity only the sound of
whiskers draining

navy blue suit and accessories ordered on
the bed fragments of you reassembled for
meetings and luncheons and meetings
agenda appended by a smile endless
reflections of you in mirrors dressing table
scent dutifully applied layers of disguise
in cloth and scent

reports between hurried bits of English
muffin notes dashed on the long yellow
paper preparations in pieces for another
day notations in a calender puzzle that only
you can decipher minutes becoming hours
becoming days pieces of you here and there
in facsimile

hurried lunch on Jasper Avenue performers
fill the walk and a harlequin dances scarlet
and green and white staring at you from behind
the mask without identity without even gender
deep set eyes catching and holding your own
an assembly of cloth and movement and
painted smiles

AT THE POLO GROUNDS

Picture New York. Summer of '39. The Giants are home
against the Boston Braves, the Polo Grounds lazy in the first
heat of summer. Men, ties loosened, daub temples, slide
on to hard slats, pencil names into another scorecard. Minor
adjustments. Scattered players slump against the playing
of the national anthem, wonder if the temperature will hit

triple digits. Everyone knows neither team is going to hit
first place, or take the field as their breath meets the cold home
air and lingers like all the little aches the coaches make you play
through as the season spirals down towards the first
days without baseball. More than a double play seems a minor
miracle, but the Polo Grounds carries on, one ritual slides

into the next. The pitcher takes the mound, throws a slider
to the lead off man. Eyes on the ball, the batter hits
the dust of the box, brushes off the red flecks, a minor
setback. And so begins the give and take of away and home,
the rhythm of the everyday. Necessary, like the run to first,
safe or out, on every touch of the bat. But ordinary plays

sometimes accumulate, become larger than any one player.
Take Johnny Cooney. Fifteen years without the ball sliding
from his bat to the stands in left, almost forever before his first
home run. Two men on, two out, and a 1-1 pitch. Cooney hits
a long drive to left, solid, like being called up from the minors
or rounding the bases at a slow trot, cleats digging for home.

Cooney knows it is gone the moment he swings across home
plate, takes two steps towards first, thinks back to all the plays,
all the swings of fifteen years. In the stands, few record this minor
triumph. The Polo Grounds has seen its share of excitement — slides,
shots to the gap, game-winning runs, years when the Giants hit
enough to win the pennant. And so this at-bat, Cooney's first

homerun in fifteen years, is scored like any other, a line from first
in pencil around the bases — second, third, and finally home.
The next day, sky clear in the late afternoon, Johnny Cooney hits
his second homerun. It must feel like a regular part of his play,
but it will be the last of a twenty year career. He will slide
into his regular play, .286 lifetime, 1172 games beyond the minors.

Picture Johnny Cooney. The first and the last in two days of play,
unknown as he walks home to his hotel, rhythm of baseball sliding
yesterday into today. Just ask him: to hit a homerun is never minor.

INERTIA

Bodies at rest,
Heineken
or Chardonnay
lightly touching
nervous fingers
remaining
always at rest.

Bodies in motion
marinated in scent,
pheremones
of happy hour
drifting in sound,
remaining
always in motion.

Veiled eyes
scour the room,
weight of expectation
increasing the frenzy,
drawing each other,
searching for that
brief encounter
that will change
motion to rest,
rest to motion.

THE FIRST AND THE LAST

Meretricious, she said, word shot straight through
my breast, her mouth a gimbal, tongue
lashing, horizontal, unwavering. I couldn't move,
stasis absolute, positioned by her revolving around
her words, controlled out of control, I am and am
not myself — I watch, feel, hear in slow motion.
She says I lack sincerity, can't commit, I've
heard it before, another failed symphony,
allegro relationships never slowing to adagio,
she takes the baton from my hand and it is over.

Come, she said, unexpected, I nodded and followed,
walking close to her, smelling her perfume,
intoxicated by this first movement with her,
unknown before words, before sound,
faster, faster, we ran through the grass, falling
down in each other's arms, her lips crushed to mine,
stopping our breath, tongues speaking directly
to one another, transmitting a signal stronger
than I could ever put into words.

Back to me, she is still, everything over but
the crying, but no one will cry, her standing
there spent, her word erasing me, my reply
stillborn, I slump to the couch, fumbling
in my pockets for my pack of Basics,
smoke to cover syllables still in the air,
cigarette to hide what I can't say to her.

TUESDAY MORNING

Tuesday comes again, it always does, bleak and gray,
ash moon sets on our breakfast — toast and burnt coffee
that's never very hot. She always adds too much milk,
thick, sweet, on top of all that sugar. Two lumps cover
the real taste of our cups, she thinks — the ember of earth
drowned in the too sweet liquid. She doesn't know I pine

for what lurks beneath those additives, sweet like burnt pine
remains of a campfire. The nights too short under gray
sleeping bags, I held her close, smells of hair and earth
soaking into every pore. The morning heat of coffee
was enough to wake her then. She sat under cover
of mountain ash, her hand waving away the milk.

Tuesdays we work at Bethany. Her idea: the milk
of our human kindness washes over all those supine
bodies. The spillage, she must think, will cover
us too, though when we're done, all I have left is gray
bile, too tired to even be black like it should, like coffee
straight out of the pot, water and beans from the earth

cooked slow over even heat, slow perfection we unearth
cup by cup. Across the room I can see her pour the milk,
delicate white eddies mixing with the hard taste of coffee.
Agitation takes the edge off both; it makes a stain even Pine-
Sol can't clean, day after expanding day, the first hint of gray
telescopes into everything and nothing can ever cover

it again. That's what happens sometimes when the cover
comes unhinged, you notice how nothing on earth
will hold its shape, how the wash comes out gray,
the best detergent, delicate cycle and still it milks
the color out all the same. She's there in her pine
tinted robe, standing by the Tuesday counter, coffee

pot in one hand, off again, not thinking about coffee
or what the sugar means or about everything that covers
what is really there — throw rugs over hardwood, the pine
air freshener suspended from the Chevy's mirror, earth
tossed over weeds and flowers. She reaches for the milk,
Tuesday morning together, the sky outside its usual gray.

Once I drank coffee and thought I would give the earth,
the moon, cover her body like a young lover, in kisses of milk,
Tuesdays fresh like alpine smoke, morning cold trailing gray.

SUSPENSION

smoke too tired
to rise above her dark
hair in the close
of heat embracing
skin memories
barely able to burn
her effigy fleeting
in the dark echoes
of sense disappearing
ember melting into
the settle of haze

DRIFT

we drift separate and syllabic
if we survive at all.
Audre Lorde, "Thaw"

1. Hank

There's just no good can come of Lettie
leaving. She isn't ready, but she thinks
she knows everything. Tilda and I tried
to raise her right. Now she won't even
hardly talk to me anymore. I remember
when she was a little girl she'd be tugging
at my pant legs, asking if it was time yet
to go out and feed the cattle and horses.
Or sometimes she would just walk with me
out in the wheat, go off between two of the
rows, and look way up to the top of the stalks.
I could hear her saying, *Daddy, they must go all*
the way to the moon. Now she just walks
away from me like I'm a piece of a photograph
instead of a man. It's like she lives in another
county, some other place that I can't ever
find, like there are no roads from there to
where I live. It's like she's floating away.

But she's so headstrong, determined to be
more and more like her grandmother every
day. I look at Lettie and it's like staring at
photos of my mother when she was a girl,
hair loose on her shoulders, me hitched
up on her hip. That might be the last time
we smiled at each other. No tears when
I left to try farming up here, just a lot of guilt
about abandoning her and father in Nebraska,
like it was selfish of me to want a life of my own
beyond the hardware store, every nail neatly
arranged in its own bin, everyone's life
according to mother's and father's plan.
How can Lettie be so much like a woman
she's never met?

2. Lettie

I told June already that Daddy won't let me
go with her, but she just keeps pushing
me. Doesn't listen to a thing he's said
to me at all, what with being so stuck on
herself. All she wants to know is what
does this mean for June Armstrong?
Sometimes I think I could be anyone and
June would be happy. Probably wishes I
was that August Rovnel, taking her off to
London or New York instead of Edmonton.
I told Daddy all about that beauty school,
showed him the letter and everything.
He just won't let go. He says it's for
my own good. He even had the nerve to ask me
what do I know about the city anyway. Doesn't
he know I listen to the programs on the radio
every night? Doesn't he know that June's cousin
told us all about it, even showed us pictures of
Jasper Avenue? I know more than he wants
me to know. Sometimes I don't even know what he's
saying. It's like when the radio doesn't come
in too well and you have to make up every second
word. You strain your ears but you never know if
what you think it says is the same as what it really
means to say. What can I say to make him understand?
Shouldn't I be able to make up my own mind? How old
do I have to be? I'm eighteen, older than Momma

when she married Daddy. He thinks I'll marry a farmer
and stay around close to them, become one of those
farm wives in the pictures, standing in front of some old
house, sour-faced with a whole passle of kids around.
I won't. I see Momma like that sometimes when I close
my eyes and then her face starts changing into mine and
I get scared. I think Momma knows, but Daddy won't
even listen. I'm not a little girl running out to check
the cows with her daddy anymore. I love him, but
I have to get to a place that's my life and not his.
He can't make me stay, he can't, even if he won't let
me go to Edmonton. How am I ever going to see
Guy Lombardo stuck way out here?

3. June

I swear I don't know why she doesn't just leave.
That's what I would do if I had parents as thick
as hers. I'd just get on that train and never look
back, wipe my feet of this place and be done. Next
stop Edmonton and no turning back. But I'm not
her, I guess. Maybe she really wants to stay here.
Who knows? Maybe she wants to live and die
and grow old and marry August Rovnel. Maybe
she doesn't really want to go to Edmonton with me.
I try to tell her about how it will be living together
without parents to tell us what to do. On our own,

just me and Lettie. We'll spend our days at beauty school and our nights out dancing. I can see us doing the Lindy on opposite sides of that big old floor, each in the arms of some beautiful Air Force Man. It'll be just like in those pictures in Life magazine. I'll work my way up to how our lives will be changed and all she can say is how her daddy won't let her go, like she has no mind of her own. I just don't understand that girl and I'm tired of it. It's her life and she can do what she wants. Me, I'm heading out to Edmonton. With or without Lettie Harris, come next week, I'll be in Edmonton, dancing with some of those Air Force Men, Guy Lombardo or somebody like that playing in the background. Let her make up her own mind. Whatever she decides, 1943 is going to be a good year for June Armstrong.

4. Tilda

Sometimes I hear Hank and Lettie fighting in the other room. All I can do is walk away. I go out to the garden, pull weeds, run my fingers through the soft dirt. It's so peaceful there, all the rows of peas and corn and snap beans, each in its own place, never trying to tell the others what to do. But not in this house. I try to help, try to reason with both of them, but neither of them wants to hear me. No one listens. It's like we're each

in our own row, separate, but yelling across to the
others even though its too far to hear what anyone
says. We live side by side but our worlds never seem
to touch. We might as well be people in a photograph,
the amount we listen. Most of the time I'm surprised
we even speak the same language; most of the time
I know we don't. I'm just tired of it, tired of how far
apart we are in this house. This fight isn't even about
going or not going to Edmonton, it's about our
lives, about the way that nobody ever listens.
Hank and Lettie are both that way
and she gets more like him everyday. All this talk
about going to Edmonton, what's it going to add
up to but more hurt, more shouting, all of us farther
apart than we ever were. How can we be whole
when we're so much apart?

THE BALLAD OF JOHN CORRIDEN

Sometimes when people find out
they want to know how it felt
to stand on second base at Ebbets Field.
Brooklyn noise all around.

Signs flashing from Durocher.
The Cardinals' pitcher stealing looks
at me watching back, the pinch
runner in scoring position.

Eddie Stanky easing up to the plate.
The rest of the Dodgers on their feet.
Dirt on Marion's pants at shortstop.
Feeling everything and nothing.

That's what it felt like to stand there,
to flex my legs, ready to run for third
and then for home. Eight years to get
to that base, a stand-in for someone else,

one hundred and eighty feet my whole
career. But no one wants to know
about the times before or after, about all
those nights on old buses, playing for four or five

hundred people, for a few dollars, for Red.
That was my father's nickname, from his playing
days with the Cubs and Tigers and Browns, before
the War, before I was born. He said he always knew

I would be a ballplayer, from the day I picked up
a ball in our front yard in Logansport through all
those days in the minors. He was there that day
in Brooklyn, somewhere on the third base side,

looking down on me, watching my career
unfold in that one game, second to third to home,
cleats scarring the perfect dirt of the infield.
One run, no at-bats, no time in the field.

EXHUMING DESIRE

It's nothing more than a problem of pathology,
how the body is consumed by disease, accident,
neglect. How it stops and no one knows how or why

until it is cut open, layers of skin, tissue peeled
back to reveal a ruptured spleen, a collapsed lung,
an exploded heart. We need science to persuade

that death is rational, can be bargained with,
explained away. We need the dead to reassure.
The answers aren't always easy, the secrets

clutched close to the chests of the dead. And so
we return to the cause, as if how people die can
explain how they lived. Together we speculate

on probable cause, armchair and professional
pathologists nosing at bodies whose flesh is long
corrupt. But sometimes the past is exhumed without

disturbing the grave, a coroner's game of circumstance.
A file, "E.P., a writer from Richmond," a brief sketch
of symptoms and Edgar Allen Poe is newly diagnosed.

Death by rabies. Telltale, the headline announces.
A sound medical hypothesis, supported by all
available data. Reconstructed with pathological

care and attention to detail. The symptoms fit
the life others wanted him to live, disprove the
mythology of cognac and roses. The sullied

flesh is redeemed, reputation resurrected by
intellectual autopsy. Clean and easy,
without mortification.

SHINNY

Days of shinny, we played pick up games far into the night
until our feet were numb, toes feeling like they would snap off,
fingers rubbing through socks soaked with sweat, kneading
the feeling back, ready for another period in the never ending
game past the moment's break.

Spring when the ice got slushy, bumps grew along the boards
where water dripped from the metal roof, deep winter when ice
was burned to a ghostly white, hard, unforgiving, knees, elbows
bruised to a fine black, shavings rising from stopping skates,
a delicious arc of ephemera.

Half-cylinder of corrugated steel, oversize machine shop becomes
a rink, men of the town coming in from the field, tractors giving
way to hammers and saws and arc welders, coming together for
us, for skating, for games of hockey on cold Canadian winter
nights that seemed to last forever.

Sitting in this southern town, no nights cold enough to frost your
moustache, I wonder if anyone knows who built our rink or what it
meant, if anyone skates or plays hockey long into the night, giving
themselves over to the game, surrendering to air thick with cold,
breath suspended for just a moment.

INHERITANCE

How do I read the guns
my father will leave,
the guns I never saw
him fire, the guns that still
lie hidden in the basement
cold room?

I can feel my father's hands
in the burnished stocks
of the shotgun and twenty-two
and see him as a young man out
shooting gophers, shooting coyotes,
hollowing out a space for himself

and his family. The man I see
is smiling, cap askew on already
thinning hair, jacket pulled up
tight against the wind, gun pointed
to the earth. Never caught in the act

of shooting. Never teaching his son
the ways of guns. There should be
traces of meaning in objects, glimpses
that speak between generations:
Here, take this, you'll need it. You

know what it means. But I wonder
what gets lost in the translation,
what deeper signs wait just below
the surface of realization.

Heirlooms are never obvious,
never objects you can pluck
from the pages of a family tree.

FOUR

CHICAGO, 1989

I remember that bar on Madison where we stopped to buy cigarettes on our way downtown. Every head turned to look when Dave and I walked in the door, five old men squinting at us over half empty glasses of draft. We pulled up to the bar and ordered a couple of Old Styles, acting like we knew. I went to the cigarette machine and bought a pack of Chesterfields, the ones with no filter, and one of the old men said, *You don't actually smoke those damn things, do you?*

I sat down beside him and we began to talk. John told me he was seventy-two and had worked on the Burlington and Northern all his life and didn't have any family. His skin was brown and cracked and his plaid shirt was badly worn at the collar. Like Al, the man who sat by Dave, John lived above the bar, on a small pension from the railroad. I looked at his worn hands and the creases in his face and asked if he regretted anything. John laughed and didn't answer directly, just took a long pull on his cigarette. Then he told me about a wife and the kids they never had. He told me about the other railroad men and the smell of the engines and the way the stars and moon shone on an Illinois winter night. But now, he said, his railroad days were gone, like her. His eyes looked past me as he finished the story and as he awoke from his memories, he recovered his hoarse laugh. I recovered my own smile and asked him the name of the bar, but he didn't know. No one knew, not even the bartender. It was just the bar and why did it need a damn name anyway?

We asked the bartender why there were upside-down shot glasses in front of our stools and he told us that John and Al had bought us a drink. We both knew they didn't have much money, but there were the two shot glasses, overturned and glittering in the pale light of the bar. We took a shot of rye and I drank to Al and John and to what I was learning I didn't know.

ONE AND COUNTING

The thing about a home run is, you never know
where or if it will ever happen again.
— Matt Williams, Giants' Third Baseman

Sometimes I wonder if the words will ever
come, pouring from my fingers, a deluge
of syntax that may never stop, but always
does. That's what it feels like when I get
in a groove and my head, my hands
feel right, like the ten-game hitting streak
where you can see every stitch rotate
towards you and you know the ball will
land with the soft squish of outfield grass.

Sometimes I hear Saturday afternoon
announcers talk about streak hitters, how
they're set in the box and every stroke connects
to the hard core of their bodies. But I never
hear anyone talk about streak poets, how
they're set with their notebooks and every stroke
of their pens connects to that same hard core.

Then the slump, the droughts of 0 for 4, games
and days that mount without a hit, without a
poem, the connection severed temporarily. At least
that's what I hope, that sensation will return,
that the rains will come again, that I will author
a hit, beat out another poem, retrieve what I've lost.

Nothing seems to work, not a change in ritual or
location, not a change in the way I'm holding
my thoughts. Sometimes it's just the mental
acrobatics that throw me off, make me swing at
a bad line break, write myself into a double play.

But I have to play through it, keep stepping into
my study, keep agonizing over words that may
never grow into poems. I must be patient at the
desk as faint glimmers of ideas carry me to the
warning track again and again. And then words
will fly just over the fielder's outstretched glove,
a stanza that feels solid as it leaves my pen, a poem
that leaves the yard, a one-game hitting streak
that feels like it will never end.

MONROVIA

table littered
styrofoam cups
plastic stir sticks
never long enough
burning your fingers
as you stir the tea
crossword puzzles
strewn below the debris
finished but for
that word that just won't
come to mind
like the capital of Liberia
or the composer of *La Traviata*
her across the table
hair flowing over black
cardigan scented with
rosewater imprint
of her lips
on the half-empty cup

PRINCESS NIGHTS

The walk to those films on Whyte Avenue
from our old house by the university, an eight block
prelude to *Casablanca* or *Annie Hall* or some other
name now lost in memory, left only the feeling that
all of it somehow meant something. I remember those
walks as always perfect, the summer nights beautiful and long,
Strathcona trees waving gently in the breeze as we walked
in evening's last light, Ostap and I talking about films and the future,
screen lives and our lives melding, evening's ferment remaining
with me through the warm days of our last summer together.

It must have rained on those Edmonton nights, conversation turning
to where to eat and whether the Eskimos beat the Stampeders,
but distilled Princess nights are what I now carry, vintage memories
of when the air was warm and the company was good.
Actualities of weather and conversation muting with age,
Ostap and I, weather perfect, is the story I tell myself.

THE MIDDLE OF AMERICA

In the middle of America it's hard to love
the carom of the puck around end boards
stained rubber black.

It's hard to spend a Saturday night without
Hockey Night in Canada, the Leafs against
the Canadiens again from the Forum.

It's hard to remember the spray of ice
shaved by blades just edged in
the rink's tiny dressing room.

It's hard to explain what it means to ice
the puck or be off-side, to break a rule
or cross a line only you know exists.

It's hard to feel the puck on the blade
of your stick, the movement from forehand
to back, the rhythm of wood on ice.

It's hard to see a sheet of ice after the first
flood of the morning, the steam rising
like your breath as you circle the goal.

It's hard to judge the distance you've come from
hamburgers and grilled onions that seemed
the same in every arena where you ever played.

It's hard to turn to the third page of the local
Sports Section, to find hockey has the same
coverage as dog racing.

It's hard to watch how the line between player
and spectator solidifies, the ball you never
carried heavier than any stick you ever held.

In the middle of America, it's hard not to love
football, invent a past, blocking sleds and nickel
defences replacing hockey sticks and power plays,
even though you can still feel the tape's rough
back as you wrap it around the heel of a new stick.

SYNCHRONY

It's not the man and woman who walk
across campus, arms trailing across

smalls of backs. It's not the way
he squeezes her hand or how

she looks up at him from beneath
brown bangs. It's not even the velvet

box he pulls from his knapsack
or how he turns shy and awkward

next to her or the way her eyes jump
wild and alive from the box to his face.

It's the way he drops to one knee,
the quick caress of March grass on

pant's crease, and how he rises to meet
her and thinks only Memorial Stadium

is there to witness. It's the way she
looks at him, cracks the hinge, catches

the gleam of stone. It's the formality,
the ritual, the way the world shrinks

to a factor of two. It's the moment
that passes between two lovers

as their lives unfold in front of your eyes.
It's a walk across the quad on a warm day.

It's how the world happens around us
whether we know it or not.

THE POSSIBLE LIFE

The body language of the mother
implies more than she could say,
the tired joy that permeates her form,
baby hitched up on her slender left
hip as she calls after the twins, five,
hell on wheels, her husband says.

She never meant for this to happen,
can't even recall how it did, but here
she is, pushing this stroller through
the first days of summer, the end of
an old rhyme, love, marriage, this
constant weight of love.

When she's older and her adult
children ask if she ever regrets
the past, she smiles, answers the
arc of their eyes with assurances,
children make it all worthwhile,
you'll see. But sometimes she admits

to herself her imagined life without
maternal love, what might have been
if the light coalesced in another pattern
of intricacy. It's just sleight of mind,
poof and they're gone, but they're never
gone far, some trap door hides them

in another part of her mind, pops them
back into the present, the possible
life that chose her.

beneath the horse's eye

the hex symbol faded against
the red of the old barn me staring
frozen through the camera lens at
the circle framing star framing painted
ebony horse head from my childhood
focus image memory focus my father
points to the freshly painted head and
star and circle and i smile at him in his
grease-stained overalls smell of the wheat
still in his pantleg barn-red tractor
noisy by the road leading to the field
i can almost see my father and me in his
arms and his father and the homestead
and i am captured too generations
implicated in flesh and i am gone from
the farm the land sold twenty years
before now i am here the barn and
the worn eye of the horse camera adding
another layer to the concentric circles
images within images
click barn circle star horse
etched in black and white

IN MISSISSIPPI

In Mississippi things would have been different,
the way the flowers drip their scent to the air.
The possibility of another life is never absent,

insects float above the blossoms, bodies bent
to capture every last drop of their sweet affair
in Mississippi. Things would have been different

if I had taken the offer, packed up, a transient
mind adrift in a life not yet formed, vaguely aware
the possibility of another life is never absent.

I never made it to Starkville, found in you the present,
a different heuristic, the re-pollination of my years.
In Mississippi things would have been different,

another life, another me, another us. My diligent
imagination turns the permutations over and over.
The possibility of another life is never absent,

only buried under layers of neglect, ever nascent.
Through the years you showed me that though
in Mississippi things would have been different,
the possibility of another life was never absent.

ROADSIDE ATTRACTION

I am always standing by the side of the road
in pictures taken at gas stations or rest stops,
my arms resting on the roof of the Sentra,
interstate miles, signs for Gas, Food, Lodging,
the rhythm of the traffic replaced by the still
of an Iowa or Wyoming or North Dakota afternoon.

We stop so that Heidi can take pictures of the landscape,
north of Minot, the sweep of the North Dakota hills
orange and red in the pale light of late afternoon.
I walk by the side of the road, uncrooking my legs from
the long drive, my back soaked from the sweat of miles.
The hood of the car is hot and I know it is time to rest.

Heidi is always absent from these roadside shots,
recording the drive with both camera and pen,
passenger side perspective balancing my own,
vinyl seats hot beneath our bare legs, wind blowing
through the opened windows of our maroon Sentra,
our movement gauged in dashboard clicks of the odometer.

I run my hand along the side of the car, the dust of southern
Sakatchewan still thick on the dark paint, masking scratches,
rust just beginning to show above the wheel, in the dent
that's been there as long as I can remember, mysterious,
a beauty mark I tell Heidi, a handsome scar she tells me
and we laugh to ourselves every time.

It was Heidi who named the car, christening it then as
part of our family, a refuge, a place to talk and plan
the coming months and years — marriage, graduate
school, moving from Alberta to Lincoln, Nebraska.
Through all the talks, there were always the three of us,
traveling, soaking up the drive for the sake of the drive.

I hear the click of the shutter, Heidi taking a picture,
us by the side of the road, North Dakota hills framing
the shot, no one but us in sight, the lonely sound of the wind
our only accompaniment. Back in the car, I pick up
the rose quartz that always rests by the dials, rubbing its pink
smoothness as I look over at Heidi and turn the key.

SAY HEY

It's hard to picture Willie Mays circa 1973.
Back in New York, the last of twenty-two
summers in the Majors, he lays on his bed,
his weathered face wet with the stream of

memories. The first time he stepped on
the field at the Polo Grounds. Jogging
from the dugout to center field, the soft
grass turning hard as August crowds

out July. The slide into second, arm
curled around the base before the tag.
How the balls of his feet touched center
field grass, anxious for another catch.

His moment of contact, wood against ball
and how it looked as it cleared the fence.
How the blue of the sky above the diamond
changes from San Francisco to New York.

How every ballpark seemed like home.
Circa 1973. Back in New York, but
the Mets aren't his Giants and the end
is nothing like the beginning or middle.

A DIFFERENT SYNTAX

Take notes. Listen to the diction of forgetting.
— Marcia Southwick, "What Should I Do?"

The Nebraska nights are long, father,
but not so long, not so deep as what
we have forgotten about each other
or, I think, what we never knew.

By sixteen I was gone from you,
three days after graduation, life
folded and packed in two new
suitcases, your way of sending

me off into the world. *Here. Go.*
There's nothing here for you.
Were those the words you spoke?
Did you say anything at all? I don't

remember, but I know that's what you
meant to say. We meant to say a lot
through the years. There's so much to
ask, to tell, to want, but we forget

the details on our few visits a year,
talk in clichés — the weather, baseball,
the latest small town gossip. I try to
remember what I do not know, questions

I mean to ask about your first love, who
you were when you were twenty-nine, who
you are now, but when we meet the words
elude me. We don't even know where to start,

can't speak the words we'll never forget.
When I leave you I never remember what
we talked about, but I do remember you,
your rough smile, your arm around my back.

Words can only hold so much; for us they
hold even less. In you I see a different
syntax I'm just beginning to understand.